Yana Goes to Kenya
By Kerubo Wall

Illustrated by
Janice Angengo

To Yana Yanushek who was a ray of sunshine;
lala salama.

Text Copyright 2022 © by Kerubo Wall. Illustrations Copyright © 2022 by Janice Angengo. All rights reserved. No part of this book may be used or reproduced in any manner whatsoever without the prior written permission of the author.

ISBN: 979-8-9867916-2-3

Today is an exciting day! **Mama**, **baba**, Noni, and I are visiting our family in Kenya.

Kenya is a **long** plane ride away.

To pass time, we read books, color, eat, watch movies, sleep, and walk up & down the aisles before we arrive.

Our first stop is the Nairobi National Park. Nairobi is Kenya's capital and the **only** city with a national park.

"The best time to see animals is early in the morning," baba says.

At the park, we see giraffes, lions, zebras, gazelles, wildebeests, ostriches, rhinos, baboons, and birds of all sorts.

Baba drives so close to a lion that we all hold our breath and hope it does not pounce on us!

Next, we drive to Nakuru.

My grandfather is so happy to see us that he gifts Noni and I a chicken!

My family has prepared delicious food.

We eat **nyama choma, ugali, mboga, chapati, mandazi, maziwa mala**, and fresh fruit.

My favorite fruit is **maembe**.

Later we play with our cousin and her friends.

We speak in Kiswahili and English.

Mama and baba decide to go on a trip to climb Mount Kenya the second highest peak in Africa.

When they get back, we ride a matatu to Lake Nakuru.

Matatus are vans that people take to work and school everyday.

They play loud music and have art on the outside.

At Lake Nakuru, we see thousands of tall, pretty, pink flamingos.

The following week, we go upcountry to visit more family.

On our way, we see fields of green plants.

"The vegetation you see is tea shrubs," grandpa tells us.

"Kenya exports a lot of tea," he adds.

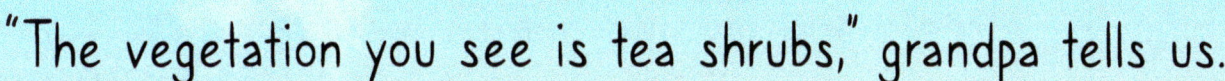

Along the streets and outside homes we see cows, chickens, goats, and sheep.

Mama points out bananas, maize and sugar cane. There are avocado, coffee, and loquat trees everywhere.

We say goodbye to grandpa's sisters and drive to the Maasai Mara for a safari.

Maasai Mara has many wild animals including The Big 5 — lions, elephants, buffalo, rhinoceros, and leopards.

Every year in July and August, over one million wildebeests, zebras and gazelles migrate from the Serengeti in Tanzania to the Maasai Mara in Kenya!

It's called The Great Migration — the **seventh wonder** of the world.

"This is awesome!" Noni shouts.

Later, we watch **Maasai** dancers.

The men jump so high and the women move their necks up and down gracefully.

Time is running out but there is still so much to see!
We take the SGR train to Mombasa to visit Fort Jesus.

It was built by the Portuguese over 400 years ago!

We eat delicious food such as **mahamri, pilau, biriani** and **sambusa**. Everyone tries **madafu**.

"It's so refreshing!" baba says.

Our final stop is my favorite — the beach in Lamu.

The sand is white and the water and skies are blue.

We play in the sand and swim in the ocean for hours.

As the sun sets we enjoy the majestic view on a dhow.

"Asante mama and baba for bringing us to Kenya!" I say and give our parents a big hug.

"Asante." Noni says and joins in the hug.

THE END

GLOSSARY

Asante - thank you

Baba - father

Biriani - similar to pilau* but the rice and meat are cooked in separate pots

Chapati - a soft, circular, thin flatbread made from unleavened wheat flour dough

Dhow - sailing vessel unique to the Red Sea and Indian Ocean

Maasai - one of the Kenyan tribes, who have preserved their cultural identity

Madafu - coconut water

Maembe - mangoes

Mahamri - similar to mandazi* but spiced with coconut milk, and cardamom

Mama - mother

*Mandazi - fried leavened dough. Great as snack, or for breakfast with chai (tea)

Matatu - public transportation vans and buses

Maziwa mala - sour milk/ buttermilk

Mboga - vegetables, usually kale/collard or indigenous leafy greens

Nyama choma - grilled meat, usually goat or beef

*Pilau - fragrant rice dish made with caramelized meat. Served on special occasions

Safari - trip or journey

Sambusa - also samosa. Triangular pastries stuffed with minced/ground beef, potato, green onions among other stuffings

SGR- a standard-gauge railway system connecting Kenyan counties

Ugali - staple food made from corn meal or millet mixed with boiling water

About the Author

Kerubo Wall was born and raised in Nairobi, Kenya. When she and her husband became parents, they knew they would teach their children Swahili. While there are numerous English children's books, there are far fewer ones in Swahili. She set out to bridge this gap with her maiden book *Yana Goes to Kenya* which will be available in Swahili and English. For more information go to kerubowall.com.

About the Illustrator

Janice Angengo is a fine artist and graphic illustrator who tells stories through visual arts and design. In her practice, she specializes in portraits and illustrations that reflect our everyday life while capturing every essence of our being. Her contribution to *Yana Goes to Kenya* is an appreciation of a country she lives in and loves to explore.

www.ingramcontent.com/pod-product-compliance
Lightning Source LLC
Chambersburg PA
CBHW042012060526
44119CB00113B/252